Koping For Kids:

A Coping Skills Program for Elementary School Children

By
Paul Lavin, Ph.D.
Kathryn Lavin, M.A.

Publisher—

Educational Media Corporation®
P.O. Box 21311
Minneapolis, MN 55421-0311

(763) 781-0088 or (800) 966-3382

www.**educationalmedia**.com

Production editor—
Don L. Sorenson

Graphic design—
Earl R. Sorenson

Cover Illustration—
Hetty Mitchell

Paul Lavin, Ph.D. and Kathryn Lavin, M.A.

Contents

About the Authors

Paul Lavin received his Ph.D. from the University of Maryland in 1971. He is currently a consulting psychologist at Norbel School in Elkridge, Maryland, which specializes in working with ADHD and learning-disabled children. Dr. Lavin has authored a number of books and articles for educators and mental health professionals who work with children and adolescents.

Kathryn Lavin received her M.A. degree from the University of Maryland and is currently a teacher in the Baltimore County Public Schools. She is the co-author of *A Comprehensive Guide for Parenting the ADHD Child* and has written numerous poems and stories for elementary school-aged children. Ms. Lavin was nominated for Teacher of the Year in 2004.

Preface

Over the past several decades, our society has become increasingly complex. Drug and alcohol abuse, family dysfunction, childhood depression, and other unresolved mental health problems plague today's youth. Our children are confronted with societal and educational challenges requiring even better decision-making and problem-solving capabilities than those of the past. Failure to learn good coping skills can have far reaching implications for the developing child. Good coping skills not only enable children to make the best use of their abilities, but they also determine whether they will become productive, contributing members of society.

Mental health and educational professionals are the logical persons to spearhead a coping skills program for children. Their knowledge of human development and their training in working with individuals and groups are the catalysts on which such programs can be built. Again, given the challenges facing our nation, it makes sense that coping skills programs should be included as integral parts of our educational planning.

The coping skills program presented in this book has been used at Norbel School in Elkridge, Maryland. Norbel School specializes in educating children diagnosed with Attention Deficit Hyperactivity Disorder (ADHD) and other learning disabilities. ADHD and learning-disabled youngsters frequently have emotional and social difficulties that interfere with their ability to learn and to interact effectively with those around them. In order to help our children address these areas, the Norbel School faculty developed an affective curriculum. This curriculum was designed so that our students could learn the cognitive and behavioral skills needed to not only overcome their deficits, but to move forward in facing future challenges. The coping skills strategies described in this book have been a part of that affective curriculum.

While some of this material was developed with ADHD and learning disabled children in mind, the overall content also would be applicable to elementary school children at almost any level. In fact, it is this broad-based appeal that motivated us to put this program together. Our goal was to make this material available to mental health and educational professionals who work with children in both regular and specialized school settings. Moreover, we believe parents could profit from using this material. The presented strategies are simple enough so that parents can teach them to their children and help them put these into practice.

As indicated previously, our coping skills program is designed to teach students to use those behavioral and cognitive skills needed to make good decisions and solve everyday problems. In order to achieve this objective, the book is organized in the following manner. First, descriptions of the basic coping skills and detailed methods for teaching them are presented. Next, a step-by-step approach shows children how to use these skills in actual practice.

The third section of the book teaches students how to role-play. This is included because the basic program requires children to actually try out the strategies they would use in coping with real-life problem situations. Because role-play is one of the best approaches for practicing what we learn, training children to effectively do this is important in implementing the overall program. It should be noted, however, that some children might already be skilled in role-playing. Therefore, they will not need to engage in the entire training sequence. Rather, only a portion may be needed with an individual child or group. Use your own judgment in this regard.

The last section of the book shows how the coping skills model can be applied in solving specific problems. A story about a boy named Dave is presented. Dave has problems understanding mathematics. Unfortunately, Dave copes so poorly that he only makes matters worse for himself. An analysis of Dave's thinking and behavior, and the strategies he might use to solve his problem, are discussed and demonstrated.

Finally, some activities that can be used to teach children to distinguish between productive and counterproductive coping strategies are presented. These should help youngsters to become more aware of the importance of acquiring good coping skills in solving both immediate and future problems.

The Basic Coping Skills Program

Introduction

In education we are concerned with the development of the whole child. However, we emphasize intellectual growth in preference to the child's social and emotional development. Although the school is the best equipped institution to teach reading, writing, and calculating, children also must be taught to deal with a variety of personal and social problems which can interfere with their capacity to learn. Youngsters with good emotional control and social skills are more likely to profit from the educational experience than children who are deficient in these areas. Unfortunately, many young people who come to school are only marginally prepared to cope with the complex social situations that occur, both inside and outside of the classroom. As a result, they may fail to cope appropriately. Such failure causes them to develop negative views of themselves, of other people, and of the educational experience as well. Of course, their negative perceptions can and often do quickly lead to mediocre or poor academic performances and problems with teachers, other adults, and peers. And, such problems can persist year after year unless significant intervention occurs in their lives.

It is our contention that teaching children to cope successfully will not only help them to view themselves and others in a more positive light, but that it will enable them to become better learners, both inside and outside of the classroom. Thus, this book focuses on helping youngsters to acquire those abilities essential in attaining improved emotional control and better interactive skills with both peers and teachers.

Before discussing the actual implementation of the program, however, two points must be taken into account. First, it is important to define what we mean by the words "coping strategy." Next, we need to distinguish between those strategies which are productive and those that are not. Once the preceding is determined, the second step requires that we identify those skills and beliefs upon which successful coping is based. This, in essence, is the model upon which our program is founded.

With regard to the first point, a coping strategy might be defined as a system of beliefs, affective responses to these beliefs, and verbal and nonverbal (body language) behaviors that we utilize in dealing with various problems as they arise. It is important to note that the quality of our beliefs, the intensity of our emotional reaction to them, and the degree of verbal and nonverbal skill that we exhibit are factors that determine whether our coping strategy will work or fail.

Effective coping strategies have two characteristics in common. They maximize the possibility that the individual will function both efficiently and productively. Efficient functioning occurs when we utilize minimal amounts of psychological energy to obtain our objectives; and productive functioning occurs when we strive to achieve goals that are both beneficial to ourselves and to those persons with whom we interact.

With ineffective coping styles, the converse appears to be true. Persons who cope inefficiently use up much of their psychological energy ruminating or worrying about dealing with potentially stressful situations. As a result, they often fail to act or they behave in a manner that is counterproductive for themselves and other people who might be involved in the situation. For example, we have all been in circumstances in which others have attempted to get us to do something that we do not really want to do. In the face of such intimidation, we may give in to their demands. This often results in us becoming angry with ourselves for "caving in" as well as becoming resentful to those persons whom we believe have bullied us. In such situations, if our ability to cope was more adequate, we might not have come off as "second best."

In fact, we might have worked out a viable compromise or just held our ground successfully. This, of course, would not only make us feel more positively about ourselves, but it would enable us to avoid much of the resentment that could become directed toward those who we perceived as being responsible for a problem, which is actually of our own making.

It is important to note that the degree of awareness that we posses regarding our habitual way of coping is a determining factor as to whether we will be able to alter our ineffective strategies. Obviously, if we are unaware as to how we typically think, feel, and behave, there is little that we can do to change our habitual unproductive courses of action. It is through education that we can enhance our self-insight and improve the quality of our coping skills. This is the theme of this book.

Model of Effective Coping

Formulating a model on what constitutes efficient and productive coping is the first step that must be undertaken before actually implementing such a program in the school. This model should consist of those cognitive, affective, and behavioral skills upon which effective coping strategies are founded. The following is a description of those skills which children must learn if they are to optimally cope with problematic situations both in and outside of school.

1. Confidence in your ability to function effectively in the problematic situation.

Persons with efficient and productive coping skills believe that they are capable of functioning successfully in a variety of situations. They are able to make positive statements (both overtly and covertly) about their potential effectiveness as problem solvers. If their behavior is not as successful as they would like it to be, they are able to utilize feedback so they can perform more efficiently and productively when entering that situation again.

2. The ability to respond to the situation with appropriate verbal and nonverbal behavior.

Persons with effective coping skills are able to use verbal and nonverbal behavior that is appropriate to the given situation. Passive, ineffectual, or aggressive behavior seldom interferes with their performance.

3. The ability to relate honestly and sincerely and to be maximally considerate of others when possible.

Persons with effective coping skills are able to express thoughts and feelings concisely and accurately so other people will know their position on matters of importance. Moreover, they are able to maintain their position without infringing on the rights of other people.

Paul Lavin, Ph.D. and Kathryn Lavin, M.A.

4. The ability to direct psychological energy (both inwardly and outwardly) so that you are optimally aware of your thoughts, feelings, and behaviors and the thoughts, feelings, and behaviors of those with whom you interact.

Persons with effective coping skills can flexibly shift their focus from themselves, to other persons, and to the environmental context without experiencing undue anxiety or threat. This enables them to concentrate on and accurately interpret all significant data that is relevant to the problem situation.

5. The ability to propose solutions or alternatives that are beneficial to yourself and to those persons with whom you interact.

Persons with effective coping skills engage in behavior, which makes it more likely that others will cooperate rather than ignore or become aggressively opposed to them.

6. Confidence that other people will be cooperative and helpful in the problematic situation.

Persons with effective coping skills believe that other people are capable of assisting in the solution of problems. Thus, they are able to make positive statements (both overtly and covertly) about their potential cooperativeness.

Summary

Persons with effective coping skills believe they are responsible for controlling the internal and external events influencing their lives. They are, therefore, able to:

1. Make positive statements about themselves, which enhance their confidence.

2. Express thoughts and feelings concisely and accurately

3. Accurately assess all components of a situation (self, others, and environmental context) and integrate this information to solve problems.

4. Make positive statements about the potential cooperativeness of other people.

5. Engage in viable verbal and nonverbal behavior in problematic situations.

6. Utilize minimum amounts of psychological energy to achieve their objectives.

Overview of the Coping Skills Program

With the preceding model in mind, the next step is to plan the program so that the children can learn those skills and attitudes essential for effective coping. In teaching these skills, it is important for children to understand that the "locus of control" for solving problems resides within each and everyone of them. In other words, they—not other people—are capable of affecting positive changes in their own lives. This objective can be achieved by teaching the children to examine the overt and covert statements that they make about themselves. For example, they may make statements such as, "I never do anything right" or "I think I can do it if I try."

Children who believe the former are likely to fail because they think that they are incompetent and that there is little they can do to change things. Children who believe the latter, however, are more likely to succeed because they think that they are capable of achieving providing that they put forth the necessary effort. Thus, the first step in our program would be to teach children to identify those productive and unproductive statements they make about *themselves,* and then to replace these negative beliefs with positive ones.

Once this has been achieved, teaching children to identify those unproductive and productive statements that they make about *other people* would be undertaken. Learning to replace the former with the latter would then follow.

The next step would be to teach children to identify and distinguish between the different types of emotion and their varying levels of intensity. Showing them how their thinking influences their feelings would then be emphasized. Following this, the children would be shown how nonverbal and verbal behavior helps or hinders them in achieving their goals. Lastly, they are taught to accurately assess all of the components of a social situation (self, others, and environmental context) so that they can use this information in planning effective ways to cope when problems arise.

In summary, the following sequence of skills should be taught in order to prepare children to become efficient and productive problem solvers to:

1. Identify and discriminate between negative and positive self-statements or beliefs and to replace the former with the latter.

2. Identify and discriminate between negative and positive statements or beliefs about other people and to replace the former with the latter.

3. Identify and distinguish between different emotions (anger, anxiety, depression) and their varying levels of intensity (annoyed, angry, furious) and show how our thoughts are responsible for the way that we feel about ourselves and others.

4. Identify and discriminate between verbal and nonverbal behavior, which is unproductive or productive in helping us to achieve our goals. For example, children can be shown that if we are annoyed with someone, the failure to make eye contact or smiling when we are expressing our thoughts actually detracts from and distorts the message we are trying to convey to him or her.

5. Analyze all of the significant components of a social situation (self, others, environmental context) and identify appropriate and inappropriate courses of action for dealing with that situation. Have the children try out appropriate verbal and nonverbal behaviors for dealing with different situations so feedback about their effectiveness can be provided.

Implementation of the Coping Skills Program

As the preceding indicates, there are five skill areas in which children must develop proficiency if they are to learn to cope efficiently and productively. The following sequence of activities can be used to teach each of these five skills. Please note that each numbered area presents activities, which coincide with the specific skills discussed in the overview section.

1. **First, teach the children that the positive or negative statements that we make about ourselves have an impact on our self-confidence. Negative statements detract from our confidence to efficiently and productively solve problems, whereas positive statements enhance this.**

We can teach the preceding by showing the child "Rob the Robot" who has a computer for a brain. (See Figure 1.) Rob can be introduced in the following ways. A picture of Rob can be given to each student. It can be drawn on the board, or it can be held up for the students to see. The children might be asked if they know what a robot is and what causes a robot to think and behave in the way that it does.

After discussing this, you can point out (if one of the youngsters has not already done so) that the robot in this picture has a computer located on his chest and this is the robot's brain. Also, it should be noted there are negative and positive self-statement buttons on the computer. When these are pushed, they cause different messages to go to Rob the Robot's head. It is these messages that lead to the sad or happy feelings shown by Rob's facial expression. At this point, ask the students if they understand how this works. Explain further if they fail to see the relationship between thoughts and feelings.

Once the preceding is understood, students can be asked to compare themselves to Rob. Ask how our brains are like computers (they process, integrate, and provide information). Show how this information, which is forwarded to our brain, leads to the positive or negative feelings that we experience about ourselves. In order to further emphasize this point, ask the children to note the buttons on their clothing and pretend that these buttons contain "good" and "bad" messages. If we push one of the "good" buttons, this sends a positive message to our brain. This results in good feelings. On the other hand, if we push a "bad" button, a negative message is transmitted to our brain. Bad feelings then follow.

In doing this exercise, emphasize that it is our belief system (the actual thoughts that we generate about ourself) that determine whether we have or lack confidence. Stress that confident persons are more likely to be better problem solvers because they have an optimistic outlook, believing that they will be successful if they make the effort. Point out that we are like Rob the Robot. When we push the unproductive self-statement buttons in our brain, we generate bad feelings. This results in a poor performance or giving up prematurely.

In order to teach children to better discriminate between unproductive and productive self-statements, Worksheet 1 (page 28) can be used. It should be noted that the definitions of unproductive and productive self-statements do not need to be given to the children, however. They are simply provided for the reader's benefit. Rather, the various statements can be reproduced and given to the group. The children can then categorize them as unproductive or productive, along with writing statements of their own into the spaces provided.

Another inexpensive technique that can be used to teach the preceding would be to have the children bring in pictures of people who are coping successfully and/or unsuccessfully. These can be gathered from newspapers, magazines, or other printed material. The children can then discuss the pictures, focusing on what the people might be saying to themselves that facilitates or detracts from their performance. Further, the children might be encouraged to keep a written log of unproductive and productive self-statements they make during the course of a day. The log page might be formatted as follows:

Situation	Productive Self-Statement	Unproductive Self-Statement	Feeling	Behavior

In using the log, the children would write down the self-statement they made and categorize it appropriately. They would then identify the situation in which the statement occurred, along with the feeling and behavior that followed. From the log, the children could determine whether they made more productive or unproductive self-statements and how these influenced their feelings and actions. Those children who are courageous enough might even share their findings with the group.

2. Second, teach the children that the negative or positive statements that we make about people influence our perceptions of them. Negative statements cause us to view people as being untrustworthy and uncooperative. Positive statements, on the other hand, cause us to view people as being potentially helpful and cooperative.

Figure I
Rob the Robot

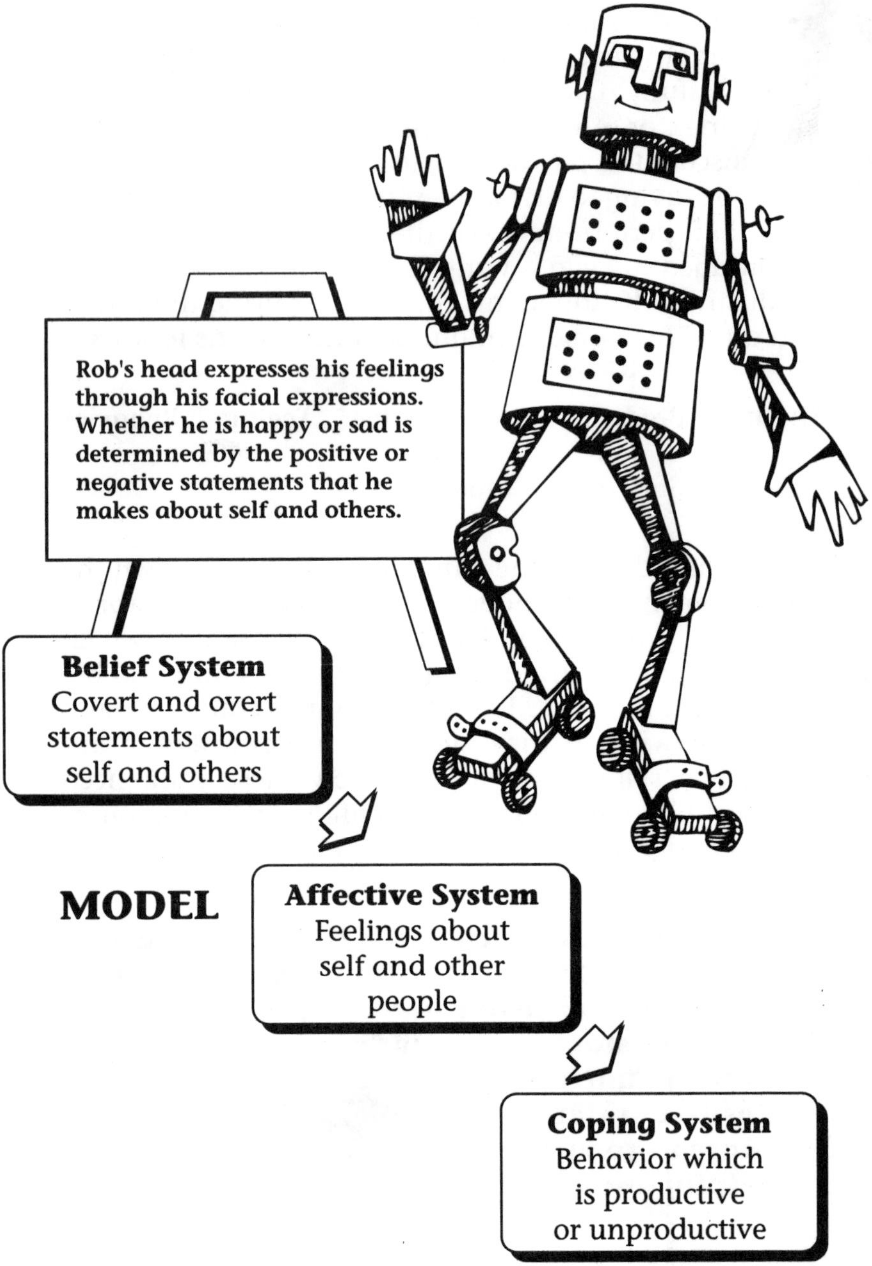

Rob's head expresses his feelings through his facial expressions. Whether he is happy or sad is determined by the positive or negative statements that he makes about self and others.

Belief System
Covert and overt
statements about
self and others

MODEL

Affective System
Feelings about
self and other
people

Coping System
Behavior which
is productive
or unproductive

Paul Lavin, Ph.D. and Kathryn Lavin, M.A.

Figure II
Rob's Computer
Positive Buttons

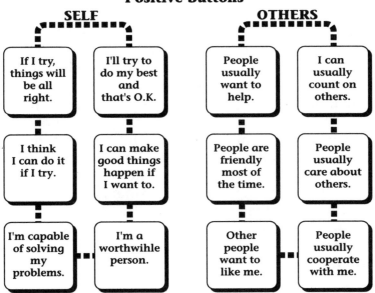

SELF		OTHERS	
If I try, things will be all right.	I'll try to do my best and that's O.K.	People usually want to help.	I can usually count on others.
I think I can do it if I try.	I can make good things happen if I want to.	People are friendly most of the time.	People usually care about others.
I'm capable of solving my problems.	I'm a worthwihle person.	Other people want to like me.	People usually cooperate with me.

Negative Buttons

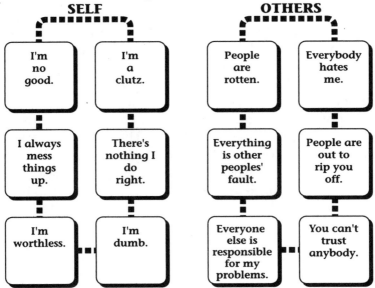

SELF		OTHERS	
I'm no good.	I'm a clutz.	People are rotten.	Everybody hates me.
I always mess things up.	There's nothing I do right.	Everything is other peoples' fault.	People are out to rip you off.
I'm worthless.	I'm dumb.	Everyone else is responsible for my problems.	You can't trust anybody.

Use Rob the Robot to demonstrate how our belief system determines our feelings and behaviors toward others. Since the children now understand how Rob's computer works, many of the introductory steps that were put into effect in phase 1 can now be eliminated. You quickly can show the relationship between the positive and negative other-statement buttons and how these influence our feelings about people. Worksheet 2 (page 29) can be used to help students to make the appropriate discriminations. The children can bring in pictures of people who are dealing productively or unproductively with others, and they can discuss what the participants might be saying to themselves that adds or detracts from their performance. The children can also keep written logs of productive and unproductive other-statements they make during the course of the day. The format would be as follows:

Situation	Productive Other-Statement	Unproductive Other-Statement	Feeling	Behavior toward others

The recording system would be the same as indicated in step 1. One other technique can be used to teach children to view other people more positively. Have the children write down those attributes they admire about other members of their group. These statements can then be deposited in a box and passed out to those youngsters who are supposed to receive them. The following format can be used: "John is generous. He is always willing to share what he has with others; Sally is a good leader. She is always organized and seems to know what needs to be done to make the class get along better."

3. Third, in order to teach the children about feelings, begin by discussing what a feeling is, the different types of feelings that we experience, and their varying levels of intensity.

Feelings can be listed on the board and the children can discuss the differences between them (anger vs. happiness, for example). Further, children can demonstrate an emotion nonverbally, while the other youngsters attempt to identify it along with the reasons for their choice.

Once this has been completed, Worksheet 3 can be used to teach the children to distinguish between different types of emotions. Hopefully, this will help them to increase their feeling-word vocabulary. On Worksheet 3, five basic feeling words are given: (1) Happy; (2) Depressed; (3) Angry; (4) Fear; and (5) Confused. Within each of these five categories, other feeling words of greater or lesser intensity are presented. On the worksheet, blank spaces are provided so that the children can write their own feeling words and place them within one of the five appropriate categories.

It should be further noted that within each of the five categories, the intensity of the accompanying emotions vary. For example, in the Anger category, the feeling words Annoyed and Furious are presented. Both of these feeling words are expressions of Anger. However, being Annoyed is the less intense version of Anger, whereas being Furious, on the other hand, is the more intense version of this emotion. The children should be aware of this so they can make adequate distinctions, not only between emotions, but also their varying degrees of expression. This can be achieved by discussing how the variations of Anger are expressed, both verbally and nonverbally. Verbal and nonverbal actual demonstrations of each of these emotions should further clarify the differences between them.

Finally, the children should be taught that emotions can help or hinder us in achieving our goals. Worksheet 3 (page 30) attempts to classify emotions as either *productive* or *unproductive*. *Productive* emotions arouse and motivate us to act in order to solve a problem. Such emotions provide the fuel that energizes our intellectual engines. However, the level of arousal that we experience always stays within reasonable parameters so we can make the best use of our problem solving capability. *Unproductive* emotions, on the other hand, are experienced in the extreme. These feelings are so intense they interfere with our ability to reason. As a result, we either fail to act or overreact to the presented situation. This is hardly conducive to good problem solving. Again, the use of Rob the Robot would be appropriate here. By using Rob, you can demonstrate that unproductive emotions can be altered by examining and changing our self and other-belief statements. In this way, we can prevent ourselves from either under or overreacting, thereby solving our problems more efficiently and productively.

4. Fourth, teach children that our verbal and nonverbal behavior can help or hinder us in communicating and achieving our goals.

For example, when annoyed about something another person has done, some people actually smile or deny they are angry while trying to get the problem resolved. The failure to communicate their concerns accurately, however, makes it less likely that other persons will change their behavior. This occurs because the offending parties will continue to be generally unaware of how their actions affect those around them. Similarly, if people compliment us and we fail to tell them that their praise pleases us (provided this is true), they may interpret our reactions as a rejection or indifference. They, therefore, are less likely to complement us in the future.

In order to teach children appropriate verbal and nonverbal skills, begin by discussing and demonstrating the unproductive and productive coping behaviors on Worksheet 4 (pages 31-32). For instance, you might talk with different people in the group, making eye contact with some, but not with others. The differences between the two approaches can be discussed by asking the children how they felt when you made eye contact or failed to look at them. Children might try this out with each other so they can make their own assessment of the difference. Once the preceding is completed, each of the other verbal and nonverbal unproductive and productive coping behaviors on Worksheet 4 can be discussed, demonstrated, and contrasted.

After the children have learned to differentiate between unproductive and productive coping behaviors, the next step would be to teach them to use verbal and nonverbal behavior, which is congruent or in-line with their thoughts and feelings. In order to do this, read the different problematic situations to the children presented on Worksheet 5 (pages 33-35). Following this, ask them to describe what they are feeling and thinking. They might also practice verbal and nonverbal behavior that accurately conveys their thoughts and feelings. In the beginning phase of this experience, you should serve as a model. In practicing verbal congruency, the use of the following structured response might be helpful: "I am happy when...; I become annoyed when..." and so forth. While doing this verbally, emphasis should be placed on practicing nonverbal behavior that coincides with the affective message.

In doing the preceding, stories also may be read to the children, and they may be asked to respond to the different characters who are presented. In fact, one child might role play the character, while the other child responds. Appropriate stories that have characters whom the students can role play and to whom they can react are found in this author's book entitled *Teaching Kids to Think Straight*, published by Hawthorne Educational Services.

5. Fifth, teach children to identify appropriate behaviors for coping with potentially problematic situations.

Begin by introducing the students to Worksheets 5, 6, 7, and 8. As noted earlier, Worksheet 5 presents problematic situations that children can analyze and to which they can learn to respond appropriately. This can be achieved by implementing the following steps. First, you or the children would read one of the situations on Worksheet 5. Next, they would make sure that they understand the problem by discussing each relevant aspect as it appears on Worksheet 6 (page 37). Once all the components of the situation have been analyzed, the children can refer to Worksheet 7 (pages 38-39). Worksheet 7 will enable them to determine the kind of coping situation that this might be. Once this has been determined, the children will refer to Worksheet 8, which provides sample productive and unproductive responses for coping with the problem situation. Please note Worksheet 8 (pages 40-43) contains blank spaces so the children can make up productive and unproductive response for coping with different situations, thereby learning to distinguish between them.

After the children have determined the appropriate categories and potential productive verbal and nonverbal responses for dealing with the Worksheet 5 situations, they can compare their analyses with those presented on Worksheet 9 (pages 44-51). The children can discuss the rationale for the categorizations and the viability of the suggested behavioral and verbal responses to each situation. Following the discussion, they can role play the potentially productive responses presented in Worksheet 9, as well as those they have developed on their own. A space in which they can write their suggestions or additions is also provided for each item on Worksheet 9. You and the observing children can give feedback and alter or try new strategies as needed. When the children become proficient in this exercise, they will be ready to begin analyzing the problematic situations that appear in their own lives.

Worksheet 1
Self-Statement/Self Belief System

Unproductive Self-Statements

Focus on the environment or others as controlling the individual. Consist of blaming statements indicating one can do little to change. These make constructive action less likely and indicate a lack of confidence to make things better.

1. *These is nothing I can do about things. No matter what I do, they will always be the same.*

2. *Nothing I do makes any difference.*

3. *If it weren't for those jerks, I'd be able to do better.*

4. *If only someone would help me, things would be all right.*

5. *No sense trying. I'll just fail.*

Productive Self-Statements

Focus on the self as the locus of control. These indicate the individual is willing to assume responsibility for his or her own behavior. These inspire the person to take action and indicate confidence in oneself.

1. *This situation is one I think I can handle.*

2. *I think I am capable of doing my best.*

3. *I'll do my best. Even if I fail, I can learn from my mistakes and do better the next time.*

4. *I have the ability to cope with this situation.*

5. *It's up to me to change things. If I want to do better, I've go to make the effort to be successful.*

Add Productive Self-Statements

6. _____
7. _____
8. _____
9. _____
10. _____

Add Productive Self-Statements

6. _____
7. _____
8. _____
9. _____
10. _____

Worksheet 2
Other-Statement/Other–Belief System

Unproductive Other-Statements

Focus on the negative characteristics of others and suggest people are not responsible and incapable of helping or contributing to the group.

1. *You can't trust anybody.*
2. *Nobody is worth it.*
3. *Everybody's out to rip you off.*
4. *Everybody is out to get you.*
5. *You've got to always watch your back.*

Productive Other-Statements

Focus on the positive characteristics of others and suggest that people are responsible and capable of helping or contributing to the group.

1. *Most people can be trusted.*
2. *People usually want to do their best.*
3. *You can usually get help when need it.*
4. *Most people can be counted upon.*
5. *Most people are friendly.*

Add Unproductive Other-Statements

6. _____
7. _____
8. _____
9. _____
10. _____

Add Productive Other-Statements

6. _____
7. _____
8. _____
9. _____
10. _____

Worksheet 3
Affective Self-System

Productive Affect

Emotions which can serve as catalysts to constructive action. Emotions that increase the probability that behavioral under (passive) or overreactions (aggression) will not occur.

Unproductive Affect

Emotions which are debilitating and prevent one from exercising rational control in problem solving. Emotions that increase the probability that withdrawal or aggressive behavior will occur.

Happy

Cheerful   Overjoyed

_____   _____

_____   _____

Depressed

Sad   Despair

_____   _____

_____   _____

Anger

Annoyed   Furious

_____   _____

_____   _____

Confused

Undecided   Overwhelmed

_____   _____

_____   _____

Fear

Nervous   Panic

_____   _____

_____   _____

Worksheet 4
Verbal and Nonverbal
Behavior Checklist

Unproductive
Nonverbal Behavior

Nonverbal behaviors which detract from the message we are trying to convey.

— looking down or away constantly; failure to make eye contact.

— crouched, hunched over body.

— rigid body position; arms folded tightly around body.

— distracting gestures; nail biting; twirling hair or clothing.

— constant shifting of feet; leg crossing; changing of body position.

— body/facial gestures not in line with verbal message and feelings (e.g., smiling when angry).

— other:

Productive
Nonverbal Behavior

Nonverbal behaviors which facilitate the communication of our thoughts and feelings.

— maintenance of eye contact.

— flexible body posture.

— appropriate body and facial gestures which are in line with the person's verbal message and feeling.

— erect standing or sitting, but comfortable body posture.

— appropriate distance between communicators.

— other: _____

Unproductive Verbal Behavior

Verbal behaviors which detract from the message we are attempting to convey.

— stammering/stuttering.
— unclear articulation.
— constant throat clearing.
— voice too low, too loud, or too rapid.
— other: _____

Productive Verbal Behavior

Verbal behaviors which accurately convey our thoughts and feelings.

— voice, pitch, and volume appropriate.
— rate of speech appropriate.
— clear articulation of words.
— other: _____

Worksheet 5
Problematic Coping Situations

1. You have won first prize for the best science project in the class. The boy who came in second approaches you. He congratulates you on winning first prize. What is the best way to cope with this situation?

2. You have purchased some new clothes and are wearing them to school for the first time. One of your friends comes up to you and tells you how nice you look. How should you respond to your friend?

3. You have been elected as the president of your class. One of your classmates congratulates you on your victory and tells you she thinks that you will be a good president. How should you respond to her?

4. It is a half-hour before classes begin. A classmate comes up to you and asks if he can copy your homework, which you completed last night. He said he didn't have time to do it. How would you cope with this situation?

5. You are outside of the school building. A friend comes up to you and offers you some pills. He tells you they will make you feel good and "high," as he calls it. Even though you like this person, you do not want to take the pills. What should you do?

6. You are the first person in line while waiting for service at the school cafeteria. Another youngster cuts in front of you without saying anything. How would you cope with this situation?

7. One of the teachers is explaining how to do a math problem by writing the problem out on the board. From the beginning of the explanation, you have been confused. You still don't understand how to solve the problem. What should you do?

8. You are a new student in the school and need to go to the principal's office to register. As you enter the building, you see a number of students walking in the hallway. You don't know how to find the principal's office. What should you do?

9. You are not sure how to complete a project that has been assigned by your teacher. You need further instruction. It is the end of the day and it is almost time to leave school. What would be the best way to cope with this problem?

10. You are player on the town's baseball team. You have been on a vacation for the past week. As a result, you have missed several practices. The coach is new to the team and you don't know him. What should you do?

11. You have been invited to a surprise birthday party for one of your new friends who just moved into the neighborhood. When you arrive at the party, you discover you don't know anyone there. Because the party is a surprise, your friend has not yet arrived. What should you do in this situation?

12. You are a new member of a club. The president wants you to introduce yourself to the members of the group and to tell them something about yourself. What would you say?

13. A new girl moves into your neighborhood. One day, while you are playing with your friends, you notice her standing around watching your group. How would you cope with this situation?

14. A new boy enters the school building. He looks around anxiously. He appears to be confused. What would you do?

15. Just before school begins, a classmate accidentally drops her books and pencils on the floor. They are scattered about. People are moving rapidly down the hall toward their classrooms. What would you do?

16. Your friend has asked you to go to a shopping mall, but you would rather go to a movie. You have told him you would rather go to the movie than the shopping mall. However, your friend keeps insisting that you go to the mall. What should you do?

17. A classmate keeps bugging you about letting her copy your homework after you have already said no several times. How should you handle the situation?

18. You are watching a television show in which you are really interested. You brother keeps insisting that you should watch another show. He argues that you would like it better than the one that you are now watching. You don't want to change the channel and have already told this to him. How would you cope with this situation?

19. You enter a group in which several people are talking. You are anxious for everyone to hear your point of view. As a result, you interrupt two people who are talking. You realize you shouldn't have done this. What should you do?

20. You have been arguing with a friend about the score of a football game. You contend that one team beat the other by fifteen points. Your friend says there was only a five-point difference in the score. You leave your friend insisting you are right. However, later on you find out your friend was correct. What should you do?

21. A friend has asked you to help her with an assignment. You gave her the directions but later discovered that the directions were wrong. What should you do?

22. You and one of your classmates ran against each other in order to be elected as a school representative. Your classmate won the election. How would you cope with the situation?

23. A friend with whom you play chess beats you for the first time. Your friend seems pleased to have finally won a game. What should you do?

24. A number of your classmates participated in an art contest at your school. You also made a poster and hoped to win the contest. However, another person whom you know won the first prize. You placed a close second. How would you cope with this situation?

Worksheet 6
Situation Formulation and Analysis

Your situational analysis should include the following:

1. A description of the problem

_____

_____

2. The place in which it happens

_____

_____

3. Who the participants are

_____

_____

4. Who says what to whom

_____

_____

5. What feelings each person is experiencing

_____

_____

6. What each person is thinking

_____

_____

Worksheet 7
Categories of Coping Situations

1. Affectionate situations:

Situations in which an affectionate or complementary response is made to you because of some good quality or skill that you possess (e.g., someone complements you on an excellent piece of work that you have done).

2. Confrontational situations:

Situations in which you believe that your rights are being violated or situations in which you disagree and want to share your thoughts about an issue (e.g., a friend has asked to copy your completed homework, or a student in your class thinks that a rule is unfair but you believe it is a good one).

3. Orienting situations:

Situations in which you are required to ask for directions, assistance, or information so you can complete a task more efficiently and effectively (e.g., asking a question in class when you are confused about solving a problem).

4. Establishing situations:

Situations in which you are required to introduce yourself and establish yourself as an individual who is a member of a social system or group (e.g., you enter a new school where nobody knows you).

5. Helping situations:

Situations in which you observe that another person needs assistance or situations in which assisting someone or sharing would be desirable (e.g., a new student enters the school and anxiously looks around).

6. Maintenance situations:

Situations in which you have made your point and taken a position, but another person keeps insisting that you are wrong, that you change, or that you do something you do not want to do (e.g., a friend keeps insisting you go to the movies, but you have homework to complete).

7. Self-fault acknowledgement situations:

Situations in which you have erred and you know that you have made a mistake (e.g., you blurt out an answer in class and realize you prevented someone else from answering the question).

8. Other acknowledgement situations:

Situations in which someone has achieved recognition for a job well done (e.g., a student wins first prize in a science fair in which you and all of your classmates have competed).

Worksheet 8
Productive and Unproductive Verbal Responses for Coping Situations

Affectionate Situations

Productive	Unproductive
Acknowledging help, concern, or effort directed by another person toward you.	Denying or failing to acknowledge another person's effort.
Thank you for....	*You didn't have to do....*
That was nice of you to....	*What did you do that for?*
I really appreciate....	*You really shouldn't have....*
You're welcome.	*That's okay.*
I'm glad I was....	*It was nothing.*

Confrontational Situations

Productive	Unproductive
Stating your opinions and feelings without degrading the other person.	Not stating your opinions and feelings or aggressively attacking or degrading the other person.
I'm annoyed and would like....	*You jerk! Why on earth....*
I don't agree because....	*Whatever you say is probably correct. I'm usually wrong.*

Maintenance Situations

Productive

Sticking to your point of view when you are convinced you are right.

That's your opinion, but I still believe....

I still believe that this is best for me.

I understand that you would like me to..., but I still....

Unproductive

Vacillating when you know you are correct or doubt that the other person is correct.

I know I shouldn't, but....

Okay. I guess it doesn't matter.

You are probably right, so....

Other-acknowledgement Situations

Productive

Complementing another person's success.

Congratulations! That was a fine....

Nice going. That was....

Unproductive

Failure to acknowledge or degrading another person's success.

That wasn't such a hot....

You were lucky that....

Establishing Situations

Productive

Interest in contributing to and being a member of the group.

Hello. My name is....

I'm new to the school. I'm Interested in....

Unproductive

Failure to project oneself as being interested in contributing to or being a member of the group.

I don't suppose you would be interested in....

Helping Situations

Productive

Assisting, sharing, enhancing, or including another person.

(Offering)
Can I help you?

(Sharing)
Would you like to use...?

Would you like some of my...?

(Complementing)
That is a nice....

That was an excellent....

(Empathizing)
I'm sorry that....

That must have hurt.

That must make you fell happy.

(Social Expansion)
Would you like to play with me?

Would you like to join us?

Unproductive

Degrading or failing to help a person who needs or requests assistance.

Don't bug me now.

No. You can't use....

I'd rather throw it away than give it to you.

That's dumb. Mine is better.

That's stupid.

Tough cookies.

Grin and bear it.

That's the way it goes.

You win some and you lose some.

Keep out!

Butt out!

Don't bother me.

Self-fault Acknowledgement Situations

Productive

Honestly acknowledging a mistake and attempting to correct it.

I'm sorry I did that. How can I...?

That was my error. What can I do...?

Unproductive

Blaming or avoiding responsibility for errors.

It wasn't my fault. He....

If she hadn't done....

Orienting Situations

Productive

Taking direct action by asking for help to solve a problem.

I'm confused. I wonder if you could help?

Could you please explain...?

Would you please show me...?

Unproductive

Persisting in erroneous behavior, doing nothing, complaining, or quitting.

To heck with....

Forget it. It's not that important anyway.

Worksheet 9
Guide for Classification of Coping Situations for Worksheet 5

Items 1, 2, 3
Affectionate Situations

1. **Nonverbal response:** Make eye contact and smile.

   Verbal response: *Thank you for complimenting me on winning first prize.*

   Suggested changes or additions:

   _____

   _____

2. **Nonverbal response:** Make eye contact and smile.

   Verbal response: *Thanks. I'm glad you like my new clothes.*

   Suggested changes or additions:

   _____

   _____

3. **Nonverbal response:** Make eye contact and smile.

   Verbal response: *Thank you. I appreciate the confidence you have in me.*

   Suggested changes or additions:

   _____

   _____

Items 4, 5, 6
Confrontive Situations

4. **Nonverbal response:** Make eye contact with firm facial and body posture.

   Verbal response: *No, (Name), I would not be comfortable letting you copy my work.*

   Suggested changes or additions:

   _____

   _____

5. **Nonverbal response:** Make eye contact with firm facial and body posture.

   Verbal response: *No, (Name), I don't want to take these even if they make you feel good.*

   Suggested changes or additions:

   _____

   _____

6. **Nonverbal response:** Make eye contact with firm facial and body posture.

   Verbal response: *I was here first. Please go to the end of the line.*

   Suggested changes or additions:

   _____

   _____

Items 7, 8, 9
Orienting Situations

7. **Nonverbal response:** Raise your hand.

   Verbal response: (Name), *I still don't understand the problem. Would you please go over your explanation again?*

   Suggested changes or additions:

   _____

   _____

8. **Nonverbal response:** Walk up to the closest student.

   Verbal response: *Would you please tell me how to get to the principal's office?*

   Suggested changes or additions:

   _____

   _____

9. **Nonverbal response:** Go up to the teacher.

   Verbal response: (Name), *I'm still not sure how to complete the assignment. Would you please explain it again?*

   Suggested changes or additions:

   _____

   _____

Items 10, 11, 12
Establishing Situations

10. **Nonverbal response:** Walk up to the coach.

    Verbal response: *Hi,* (Name). *My name is* (Name). *I'm the player who was on vacation last week and missed practice.*

    Suggested changes or additions:

    _____

    _____

11. **Nonverbal response:** Go up to someone and introduce yourself.

    Verbal response: *Hi, my name is* (Name). *I'm* (Name)*'s friend and I was invited to the surprise party. What's your name? How did you get to know* (Name)?

    Suggested changes or additions:

    _____

    _____

12. **Nonverbal response:** Stand and make eye contact with the group.

    Verbal response: *My name is* (Name). *I'm the new member of the club. I go to* (Name) *school and I am* (tell something about you).

    Suggested changes or additions:

    _____

    _____

Items 13, 14, 15
Helping Situations

13. **Nonverbal response:** Go up to the new person.

    Verbal response: *Hi, my name is* (Name). *What's your name? Would you like to join our group?*

    Suggested changes or additions:

    _____

    _____

14. **Nonverbal response:** Go up to the person.

    Verbal response: *My name is* (Name). *Is there anything I can do to help you?*

    Suggested changes or additions:

    _____

    _____

15. **Nonverbal response:** Stop and offer to help.

    Verbal response: *Can I help you to get your books and pencils together?*

    Suggested changes or additions:

    _____

    _____

Items 16, 17, 18
Maintenance Situations

16. **Nonverbal response:** Make eye contact with firm facial expression.

    Verbal response: *I know that you want me to go to the store with you, but I prefer to go to the movies. I wish you would stop insisting I go with you.*

    Suggested changes or additions:

    _____

    _____

17. **Nonverbal response:** Make eye contact with firm facial expression.

    Verbal response: *Look, (Name), I've already said no several times. I wish you'd stop bugging me because I'm not going to let you copy my work.*

    Suggested changes or additions:

    _____

    _____

18. **Nonverbal response:** Make eye contact with firm facial expression.

    Verbal response: *Look, (Name). I've already said I want to finish watching this TV. show. I was watching this show first. You'll just have to wait your turn.*

    Suggested changes or additions:

    _____

    _____

Items 19, 20, 21
Self-fault Acknowledgment Situations

19. **Nonverbal response:** Look directly at the person and make eye contact.

    Verbal response: *I'm sorry I interrupted you. Please continue with what you were saying.*

    Suggested changes or additions:

    _____

    _____

20. **Nonverbal response:** Call your friend to apologize.

    Verbal response: (Name of friend), *This is* (Name). *I want to apologize for insisting I was correct about the score. You were right. There was only a five point difference.*

    Suggested changes or additions:

    _____

    _____

21. **Nonverbal response:** Call immediately to correct the error.

    Verbal response: (Name of friend), *This is* (Name). *I'm sorry I gave you the wrong directions. I hope this didn't cause you any extra work. The correct directions are* (give directions).

    Suggested changes or additions:

    _____

    _____

Items 22, 23, 24
Other Acknowledgment Situations

22. **Nonverbal response:** Go up to your classmate. Make eye contact.

    Verbal response: (Name), *congratulations on winning the election.*

    Suggested changes or additions:

    _____

    _____

23. **Nonverbal response:** Make eye contact and smile.

    Verbal response: *You played very well. Good game.*

    Suggested changes or additions:

    _____

    _____

24. **Nonverbal response:** Go up to your classmate. Make eye contact.

    Verbal response: (Name) , *congratulations on winning the art contest.*

    Suggested changes or additions:

    _____

    _____

The Coping Strategies Program as a Group Guidance Activity

Paul Lavin, Ph.D. and Kathryn Lavin, M.A.

Steps for Putting
Coping Strategies Into Practice

Once the children have mastered the basic coping skills, the next step would be to provide them with the opportunity to apply what they have learned in analyzing and proposing solutions to the potentially problematic situations in their own lives. The steps for implementing this phase of the program are as follows:

1. First, write a description of the situation (See Worksheets 6 & 7), specifying the environmental context, the person or persons involved, the particular problem encountered, and any significant thoughts, feelings, behavior, or dialogue important in understanding the situation. It might be helpful to have the participants role play and record the situation on audio or video tape if possible.

2. Second, identify all of the alternative actions that might put into practice in dealing with the problem.

3. Third, place all of the alternative actions into one of three categories:

   (a) constructive, appropriate, responsible types of action;

   (b) destructive, inappropriate, irresponsible types of action;

   (c) non-action responses or responses that are neither constructive or destructive but fail to address or resolve the problem.

   In placing the responses into categories, it would be helpful to identify possible outcomes for yourself and others that will occur if you engage in the behavior.

4. Fourth, once the constructive responses are identified, determine which is most appropriate and specify verbal and nonverbal behaviors (e.g., smiling, gesturing, and so forth) that would help to make the strategy successful in this situation. Any emotional responses, positive self-statements, or positive other-statements to be utilized may be included. (See Worksheets 1, 2, 3, 4, & 8.)

5. Fifth, role play constructive responses with a partner or partners and obtain feedback regarding their effectiveness. If audio or video equipment is available, this might be utilized.

6. Sixth, once feedback has been received, make any necessary alterations in the strategy until success has been achieved.

Preparation for Role Play

Introduction

Since the children will be asked to role play, it might be necessary to prepare them for this experience by having them engage in a sequence of imaginary, nonverbal, and verbal activities. Although many elementary school children are not deterred by the inhibitions that plague adolescents and adults, nevertheless, the suggested **Preparation for Role Playing** program might be helpful since it is designed to develop the imaginary and nonverbal and verbal flexibility and spontaneity essential to effective role playing. Before initiating these activities, however, it would be best to discuss the goals of the program and the importance of group cooperation with the children. Thus, you should first read the **Preparing Children to Give Feedback** and the **Preparation** sections, which follow before implementing the preparatory role playing activities. Once this is completed, the preparatory program can be put into effect.

Preparing Children
to Give Feedback

Before initiating any role playing activities, point out that you want everyone to learn and to have fun doing these exercises. Thus, it is important the children be trained in how to give appropriate feedback to the role players. Saying, "That's no good," or "That is dumb, stupid etc." only creates inhibitions in the group and prevents children from taking the kinds of risks essential for effective role playing. Therefore, in giving feedback, the children should emphasize what they thought was good about the role play and make specific suggestions for the improvement of a strategy.

Paul Lavin, Ph.D. and Kathryn Lavin, M.A.

In order to implement the preceding, you might make a list (with the help of the group) of the things we *do not* do when observing or talking about an individual or group dramatization. Also, devise a list of things we *should do*. Examples of the former would be laughing, giggling, or making such comments as, "That's crazy, no good, etc." Examples of the latter would be looking directly at the person and listening to him or her, or telling the role player what you like about his or her dramatization (e.g., "I liked the way you smiled when you were showing what it means to be happy"). An example of giving a specific suggestion for improvement that would be helpful would be: "Your demonstration of anger would have been better if you raised your voice and made it more forceful." As just indicated, the appropriate rules for giving feedback and the list of *do's* and *don'ts* should be made in cooperation with the group. If the children participate in making the rules, they are more likely to adhere to them.

Preparation

You must be prepared to participate in this experience and demonstrate how you would portray different feelings, characters, and role plays. Hopefully, you will be able to model the kind of spontaneity you would like to see with your group. It might be helpful to try out a few of the roles in preparation for the exercises. View yourself in a mirror as you try different experiences.

Role Playing Skills

In order to prepare children for role playing, you will need to help them acquire the following skills in sequence: (1) the ability to relax; (2) the ability to utilize his or her imagination; (3) the ability to use the body's motor capabilities flexibly and spontaneously; and (4) the ability to verbalize spontaneously.

Relaxation Training

In order to teach children to relax and to begin training them to use their imagination, the following exercises might be helpful. If possible, have them lie on the floor. (Old sheets, flattened cardboard boxes, or mats could be placed on the floor to keep them from getting dirty.) If this is not feasible, they can sit in their chairs with both feet on the floor, their heads upright, and their hands on their thighs.

The first step in this procedure is to train them to breathe properly, since this facilitates relaxation. Begin by showing them how to take a deep breath, to exhale, and to follow with slow, regular breathing. In order to demonstrate this, state the following: "The first thing that we are going to do is to learn how our breathing can help us to relax. Let's pretend your chest is like a balloon that has not been filled. Let's fill it with air like this (demonstrate by deeply inhaling) and now let the air out like this (demonstrate by exhaling). Now concentrate on your breathing, letting it be slow and regular. Notice how your body relaxes. Let your breathing be slow and regular. Let yourself become deeply relaxed."

Once they have mastered the deep breathing exercise, have them close their eyes and pretend they are a floppy stuffed toy, such as a Raggedy Ann Doll or Teddy Bear, and then suggest they relax. While they are closing their eyes and pretending, walk around the room and tell them that they are becoming floppier and floppier while relaxing. Tell them you are going to raise and lower their arms while they are relaxing in order to see just how floppy they can be. If the children are having some difficulty relaxing, have them tense various muscle groups and then relax them. This can then be followed with further suggestions of relaxation. The tension-relaxation patter that might be used is presented in the next section.

Other imaginary sequences that might facilitate relaxation would be pretending they are fluffy clouds in the sky, and as the wind blows them along, they become fluffier and fluffier. Or they may pretend to be big balls of cotton, and as they grow, they become softer and softer. While these activities are occurring, walk around the room, suggesting greater relaxation and lifting and lowering arms and legs to see how fluffy and soft the children have become.

Before initiating the preceding activity, however, be prepared to demonstrate what it would be like to be a floppy Teddy Bear or Raggedy Ann Doll. Also, be prepared to demonstrate the deep breathing skills and the tension-relaxation sequence. The children could then discuss what it is like to be relaxed. This will hopefully motivate them to participate fully in the activities.

Tension-Relaxation Patter

The tension-relaxation patter that can be used is stated as follows:

Let's begin by taking a deep breath. First pretend that your chest is like an unfilled balloon. Fill the balloon with air like this (demonstrate) and now let the air out like this (demonstrate). Try it. Inhale. Exhale. Now let your breathing become slow and regular.

Now let's make your arms and fists like hammers. (Demonstrate by extending your arms in front of you in a horizontal position; then clench your fists and tighten them so that the hands, forearms, and biceps are in a rigid position.) Tighten your arms and fists. Tighten them! (Have them tense these muscles for 5 seconds.) Relax. (Have the children quickly release the tension and relax the muscles.) Just let your arms become loose and floppy. Notice the difference when your arms are like steel hammers and when they are relaxed. Let them become looser and looser, floppier and floppier. Let them become like rubber—loose and rubbery—floppier and more relaxed—deeply relaxed. Notice your breathing when you are relaxed. It's slow and regular—slow and regular. (Patter for 30 to 40 seconds.)

Now let's tighten your facial muscles. Make an exaggerated smile with your mouth so your jaw muscles are tensed. This is a bunny rabbit face. Everybody make a bunny rabbit face. Make it tight, tighter, tighter! Now let your face relax. Let your forehead, nose, cheeks, and jaw muscles wind down and become more deeply relaxed. Just let them become loose and rubbery. Let them become softer and softer and more relaxed—more deeply and deeply relaxed. Concentrate on your breathing—slow and regular. Make it slow and regular and allow your face to become more deeply relaxed.

Now let's tighten your neck muscles. Pretend that you are a turtle and that you are pulling your head into your shell like this. (Demonstrate by pulling your head down to your shoulders.) Try it. Tighten your neck inside of the shell—tighten it more and more—tighter and tighter! Relax. Let your neck come out of the shell and let it relax. Allow the neck muscles to become softer and softer—looser and looser and more relaxed—more deeply relaxed. Let your breathing become slow and regular—more and more relaxed. Just let the muscles wind down further and further and become loose and relaxed.

Now let's tense our shoulders, chest, and stomach muscles like this. Pretend that you are a big bear and that you have your arms wrapped around a tree and you are trying to root it out of the ground. (Demonstrate by folding and crossing your arms in front of you as if a tree were in the middle; then tighten your shoulders, chest, and stomach as if you were attempting to pull it out.) Everybody squeeze the tree. Squeeze it tighter and tighter! Now relax. Just let your shoulders, arms, chest, and stomach relax. Let the muscles become loose and rubbery. Concentrate on your breathing and let it become slow and regular. Let the muscles wind down further and further and become more relaxed— deeply relaxed. Allow the shoulder muscles, chest muscles, and stomach muscles to become looser and looser and more deeply and deeply relaxed.

Now lets tighten all the muscles in our legs. Tighten the thighs, calves, and foot muscles like this. (Demonstrate by lifting your legs slightly and extending them forward; then point your toes forward and squeeze them downward.) Do it now. Make your legs like steel rods. Make them tighter and tighter. Tighter! Now relax. Just let your legs become loose and rubbery—more rubbery and more relaxed— further and further relaxed. Allow your leg muscles to become looser, softer, and more deeply relaxed.

Now let your whole body relax. Just close your eyes and listen to my voice. Let your arms become loose and rubbery. Let them wind down further and further and become more relaxed. Allow all the muscles of your face to become more relaxed—forehead, cheeks, nose, and jaw. Let them wind down, loosen, up, and become more relaxed—deeply relaxed. Let your neck muscles loosen up and to wind down and become more relaxed. Let your breathing become slow and regular—slow, regular breathing. Let your shoulder muscles, chest muscles, and stomach muscles loosen up and relax. Let these muscles wind down, smooth out, and become more deeply and deeply relaxed. Allow the thighs, calves, and foot muscles to relax. Let all the leg muscles relax, wind down, and smooth out—deeply and more deeply relaxed. Let your whole body wind down further and further. Now just enjoy relaxing for a few seconds. (Let 15 seconds pass.) Now I am going to count backward from 3. When I say 3, move your legs; on 2 stretch your arms; and on 1 open your eyes and sit up straight. Ready—3 (Pause)—2 (Pause)—1 (Pause).

Imagination Training Sequence

In developing their imagination, the children might be asked to begin to visualize single step scenes and then move to more complex multi-sequential scenes as the training progresses. First, the floppy toy scenes and the cloud and cotton scenes, which were mentioned previously, might be utilized. After imagining these, the children should open their eyes and discuss what they visualized and how they felt while they were engaging in this activity. Some sample questions that might be asked are: "Describe what the floppy doll, bear, and so forth looked like? What did it feel like to be a floppy doll, bear, and so forth?" Other single step scenes that the children could practice imagining are as follows:

1. An airplane flying through some white clouds on a sunny spring day or an airplane flying through storm clouds with lightening flashing about.
2. Doing something that they really enjoy.
3. A police car or fire engine going down the street.
4. A favorite animal doing something.

You can devise other kinds of simple single step scenes that children can visualize and discuss. This should prepare the children for visualizing multi-sequential scenes in preparation for role playing. Some multi-sequential imaginary scenes that might be used are as follows:

1. Imagine you are a large bear walking through the forest. As you are walking between the trees, you notice there are some bees coming from a hole in a large tree near a stream. You walk toward the tree and notice a large yellow honey nest inside of the hole and you can almost taste and smell the honey, which is dripping from the combs in the tree. Your mouth begins to water. You reach inside the tree, take out the honeycomb, and start to eat it. It tastes good and sweet. But, the bees get very upset and fly out of the nest after you. You drop the honeycomb and run away before the bees can land on you.

2. You are a big beautiful tree in a city park. You are tall and have flowing branches with many large green leaves. One sunny afternoon, you see two small birds flying near you. You call to the birds and tell them to come build a nest in your branches. The birds come to you and land on a branch. They chirp and fly to the ground and pick up pieces of straw. They fly back and forth until they have built a large nest on your top branch. The two birds lie down in the nest and go to sleep.

Once the multi-sequential scenes, which are impersonal, are completed, you would then move to visualizing scenes in which the children imagine themselves engaging in single step and multi-sequential activities. Single step scenes which might be used are as follows:

1. Pretend that you are sitting at a table looking at your favorite desert and preparing to eat it.

2. Pretend you are sitting in a chair at home showing your parents a school paper on which you earned an excellent grade.

Some multi-sequential scenes that might be used are as follows:

1. You have just finished school and are walking out of the school building. As you leave the school area, you walk toward an ice cream store, which is nearby. You go into the store and ask the person behind the counter to give you a large scoop of your favorite ice cream. When you receive the ice cream, you pay the clerk. Then you sit down at a table slowly eating the ice cream and enjoying the taste.

2. You are at home eating dinner with your family. Your mother has prepared your favorite foods and you are enjoying eating them. After eating the main part of the meal, your mother brings out your favorite desert and you eat it, enjoying each bite you put into your mouth. After finishing the desert, you get up from the table and go over to your mother and tell her how much you enjoyed the meal. Then you and your family leave the room.

Nonverbal Training Sequence

Prior to implementing the activities in this phase of the program, have the children close their eyes and imagine themselves engaging successfully in the activity. The following are designed to help the children to use their bodies in conveying nonverbal messages effectively. These activities can be performed individually or in groups.

1. Have the children make a list of feeling words. List these on the board (e.g. angry, happy, sad etc.). Ask different members of the group to demonstrate one of these emotions. The class can then try to guess what emotion the individual is attempting to convey and they can discuss the nonverbal components that make up that emotion. You might use a timer to see how quickly the group is able to accurately guess the emotion being portrayed.

2. The previous activity might be done by having the children divide themselves into groups of four or five. They can then choose an emotion they would to portray. Each group will decide how to dramatize the emotion. Once this has been decided, they can present the emotion to the group, which will attempt to identify it.

3. Individuals or groups of four or five can be assigned the task of portraying a television show or a television personality. The group can then role play this nonverbally, while the class attempts to identify the show and the television personality associated with it. This same activity can be done using comic strip characters, super heroes, storybook characters, celebrities, and so forth. The children might also dramatize a television commercial, while the class attempts to identify the product the commercial represents.

4. The previous task might be made even more difficult by devising categories for each interpersonal role play. For example, the categories might be listed on the board as follows: (1) sports; (2) commercials; (3) comic strip characters; (4) news events; (5) storybook characters; (6) and television shows. The observers would first try to guess the category and then the event or person associated with it. Timing how long it takes to make a correct identification could heighten enthusiasm for the activity.

5 Have individual children or a group choose a particular animal and dramatize the animal doing something. This might also be done with a flower, tree, and so forth. The class would then try to guess what is being portrayed.

Nonverbal and
Verbal Training Sequence

All of the previous activities in the nonverbal sequence might be utilized in this phase of the training. However, the children would now be allowed to use words while dramatizing. It should be noted that the children should be careful not to use words that specifically identify the person, event, or thing being portrayed, for obvious reasons. Also, when preparing this material the children should make up their own dialogue. Some other activities other than the preceding are as follows:

1. The children can break into groups of four or five and play a sequence from a particular story, such as *The Three Little Pigs* or *Hansel and Gretel.*

2. The children can divide into pairs and plan how they might play these roles: (a) a small child who wants an older brother or sister to do something; (b) an angry mother or father who finds that a child has not fulfilled some responsibility; (c) a child who is lost and wants to get directions from a police officer; (d) a child who finds that his or her toy is broken because it was poorly made and wants to return it to the store where it was purchased. You or the group might make up other sequences.

The Coping Strategies Program in Action

Applying the Program
Using Anecdotes and Stories

As indicated in the Basic Coping Skills chapter, you must first train children in the following sequence of skills in order to prepare them to cope efficiently and productively.

1. The identification and discrimination between positive and negative self-statements or beliefs.

2. The identification and discrimination between positive and negative beliefs about other people.

3. The identification and discrimination between emotions which can be a catalyst to productive action and those which can be debilitating or potentially destructive to good problem solving.

4. The identification and discrimination between verbal and nonverbal behaviors which are both productive and unproductive in helping us to achieve our goals.

5. The analysis of all significant factors influencing a situation and evaluation of both appropriate and inappropriate courses of action for coping with that situation.

In order to acquire these skills, children can be taught to analyze stories, biographies, movies, newspaper accounts, periodicals, and other media presentations. For example, as noted earlier, this author has written a book of children's stories (*Teaching Kids to Think Straight*) in which the main characters fail to cope efficiently and productively with a variety of different problems. The failure to cope successfully leads to negative consequences of both an immediate and long-term nature. Such stories and anecdotes from the media can be presented to the children. After reading, listening to, or viewing these, the children can then analyze their content using Rob the Robot model and the various worksheets presented previously.

In this chapter, a story entitled *Dave Drops Out* will be presented. Dave has difficulty understanding mathematics. Unfortunately, Dave's negative thinking, his emotional overreactions, and his counterproductive behavior interfere with his ability to overcome this problem. In fact, Dave's inability to cope effectively only makes matters worse. An analysis of Dave's inability to cope satisfactorily using the materials and worksheets will follow the story. The purpose of this is to demonstrate how these can be applied with children in a group guidance setting. When the analysis of Dave's counterproductive coping style is completed, productive strategies that Dave could employ to solve his problem will be provided.

The last section of this chapter contains a list of activities and suggestions you might try in order to teach children to become more skilled in analyzing and solving problems. These activities and suggestions can be implemented in the school and community and require only a minimum of materials and expense.

Dave Drops Out

Dave was sitting upright in his chair. He was staring at the board while his teacher was explaining last night's homework assignment in mathematics. Although Dave looked like he was listening, he hardly heard anything that the teacher was saying. Rather, Dave was thinking about how difficult the math assignment had been. "Math is impossible," Dave thought. "It just can't be done," he mussed to himself.

Dave tried to listen, but he just couldn't make himself pay attention. The more he thought about how hard math was, the angrier he became. "Math shouldn't be so hard. It's unfair that one subject has to be so difficult," Dave said to himself.

Dave felt like screaming at the teacher. "Teachers are jerks! They just assign homework to ruin your life. Homework is stupid!" Dave thought. Dave began blaming the teacher and the homework because he didn't understand math.

No matter how hard Dave tried, he continued to have difficulty paying attention to his teacher's explanation. As she was talking, his eyes narrowed and a surly look appeared on his face. Dave began to sigh out loud. He started looking out of the window and began tapping his feet on the floor. Dave was becoming increasingly frustrated because he could not understand what the teacher was talking about. It all seemed like gibberish to him.

After awhile, Dave's behavior became disruptive. The teacher stopped the lesson and asked him if he was having a problem. "No!" Dave howled in a somewhat nasty, defiant tone. "She probably wouldn't take the time to explain it to me anyway," he thought to himself.

"If you are not having a problem, please pay attention," the teacher said. Dave reluctantly complied with her request. He stopped tapping his feet and glaring out of the window. He simply stared blankly at the teacher and the board even though he was still not listening.

As the math lesson progressed, Dave started to get depressed. He looked around at the other students in the class. "Look at the way that they are paying attention," he thought. "They obviously know what is going on. I'm probably the only one in the whole class that doesn't understand math. That just proves how stupid I am," Dave said to himself.

In reality, however, Dave was actually a very good student. He earned all A and B grades. While he was telling himself how dumb he was, Dave glanced down at his desk and noticed his Science paper with a grade of A on it. The teacher had returned these test papers to the class before the math lesson began. "That A was just luck," Dave said to himself. "Science is easy. If I was smart, math would be easy too."

By the time the lesson was completed, Dave had become so despondent he failed to hear anything she had talked about. His teacher had assigned homework, but Dave missed what she had said. "Forget it," Dave said to himself. "I'll just not do it. It's probably too difficult anyway."

Dave continued to look off into space. As the class prepared to leave the room, he put his head down on the desk and pretended to be sleeping. Only when his teacher prodded him did Dave get up, take his books out, and slowly move from his seat toward the door. Finally, after she reprimanded him, he left the room with a smirk on his face. "That will teach her to aggravate me," Dave said to himself as he left the room.

Analysis of Dave's
Unproductive Coping Skills

Dave produced a number of negative thoughts, which hampered him in dealing with his math problem. As indicated previously, unproductive self-beliefs are those that focus on the environment as controlling the person's life. Such beliefs consist of self-depreciating or blaming statements, indicating that one can do little or nothing to change things. They show that the person lacks confidence. Dave's negative beliefs about himself and his circumstances, which can be applied to Worksheet No.1, are as follows:

1. Math is impossible.

2. It (math) just can't be done.

3. Math shouldn't be so hard.

4. It's unfair that one subject should be so difficult.

5. Homework is stupid.

6. That (other students appearing to understand math) just proves how stupid I am.

7. That (the A science grade) was just luck.

8. Science is easy. If I was smart, math would be easy too.

9. I'll just not do it (homework). It's probably too difficult anyway.

A sample of Worksheet 1 and their insertions are as follows:

Worksheet 1
Self-Statements/Self-Belief System

Unproductive	**Productive**

Unproductive

1. Math is impossible.

2. It (math) just can't be done.

3. Math shouldn't be so hard.

4. It's unfair that one subject should be so difficult.

5. Homework is stupid.

6. That (other kids appearing to understand math) just proves how stupid I am.

7. That (the A science grade) was just luck.

8. Science is easy. If I was smart, math would be easy too.

9. I'll just not do it (homework). It's probably too difficult anyway.

Beside the negative thoughts about himself and his perceived inability to cope with math, David also thinks a number of negative thoughts about other people. As indicated previously, unproductive other beliefs are those indicating that people are generally uncaring, irresponsible, untrustworthy, and unwilling to be helpful. David's unproductive other beliefs, which can be applied to Worksheet 2, are as follows:

1. Teachers are jerks!

2. They (teachers) just assign homework to ruin your life.

3. She (the teacher) probably wouldn't take the time to explain it (the homework) to me anyway.

4. They (other students) probably know what is going on. I'm probably the only one in the whole class who doesn't understand math.

5. That (Dave's slow moving behavior) will teach her to aggravate me.

A sample of Worksheet 2 and their insertions are as follows.

Worksheet 2

Other Statement/Other Belief System

Unproductive	**Productive**

Unproductive

1. *Teachers are jerks!*

2. *They* (teachers) *just assign homework to ruin your life.*

3. *She* (the teacher) *probably wouldn't take the time to explain it* (homework) *to me anyway.*

4. *They* (other children) *probably know what's going on. I'm probably the only one in the whole class who doesn't understand math.*

5. *That* (Dave's slow moving behavior) *will teach her to aggravate me.*

Throughout the story, Dave's negative emotions become so intense that he is unable to concentrate. These are caused by the repetitive, unproductive statements that he makes about himself, his situation, and his teacher. As indicated previously, our affect becomes unproductive when it interferes with our ability to behave appropriately and to solve problems. For instance, Dave experiences increasing anger because he believes that "Math is too hard" and that "Teachers are jerks!" He becomes overly frustrated because he cannot concentrate in order to understand the teacher's explanations. Again, this is the result of Dave's negative thinking.

Eventually, Dave becomes depressed. He concludes that he is "stupid" and that everyone else understands the work. He believes that he is alone in not understanding math. Dave's unproductive emotions, which can be applied to Worksheet 3, are as follows:

1. Increasing anger
2. Overly frustrated
3. Depression

Worksheet 3
Affective Self-System

Productive	**Unproductive**
	Happy
Cheerful	Overjoyed
_____	_____
_____	_____
	Sad
Sorry	Despair
_____	*Depression*
_____	_____
	Angry
Annoyed	Furious
_____	*Increasing Anger*
_____	_____
	Confused
Undecided	Overwhelmed
_____	*Overly Frustrated*
_____	_____
	Fear
Nervous	Panic
_____	_____
_____	_____

Finally, Dave's unproductive thinking and emotions caused him to behave badly. As indicated previously, unproductive behavior interferes with our ability to communicate and to constructively solve problems. For instance, Dave's frustration led to the following inappropriate behavior:

1. A lack of concentration.

2. The narrowing of his eyes and a surly look upon his face.

3. Sighing; looking out of the window; and tapping his feet on the floor.

4. A nasty, defiant tone of voice.

5. Saying "No" when the teacher asked if he was having a problem.

6. Putting his head on the desk and pretending to sleep.

7. Moving slowly from his seat toward the door.

Dave's unproductive verbal and nonverbal behavior, which can be applied to Worksheet 4, are inserted as follows:

Worksheet 4
Verbal and Nonverbal Behavior Check List

Nonverbal Coping Behavior

Unproductive	Productive

Unproductive

1. A lack of concentration.
2. The narrowing of his eyes and surly look on his face.
3. Sighing.
4, Looking out of the window.
5. Tapping his feet.
6. Putting his head on the desk and pretending to sleep.
7. Moving slowly from his seat to the door.

Verbal Coping Behavior

Unproductive	Productive

Unproductive

1. Saying "No" when the teacher asked if he was having a problem.
2. A nasty, defiant tone of voice.

As the preceding demonstrates, Worksheets 1, 2, 3, and 4 can be used to examine the distorted thinking, emotional over-reactions, and unproductive behaviors that were responsible for Dave's inability to cope in this story. In conjunction with using the worksheets, you can utilize the Rob the Robot model to show how Dave's thinking contributed to his emotional over-reactions and inappropriate behavior. The latter would be particularly effective in working with younger elementary school children.

Teaching Dave
to Cope Productively

As indicated at the beginning of this chapter, an analysis and description of how Dave might be helped to cope productively utilizing the text material would be presented. After identifying Dave's self-defeating thoughts, helping Dave to develop productive beliefs to replace these needs to be undertaken. Productive self-statements Dave might use to challenge his unproductive thoughts are as follows:

1. It is certainly possible to learn math. Many other people have done it.

2. Math is difficult for me and it will require more effort. I can master it if I am willing to try.

3. The difficulty of a subject has nothing to do with being fair. Some subjects are naturally more difficult than others.

4. Homework is assigned so that you can practice and reinforce what you learn in class.

5. Just because other people are listening doesn't mean they aren't having difficulty, nor does it mean I'm stupid. It just means I'm having trouble understanding math. If I am willing to try, I can understand it.

6. I earned the A in science because I was able to correctly answer the questions. I deserved the A.

7. Science is easier for me than math. Because one subject is more difficult than another doesn't mean that I'm not smart.

8. I can probably do the homework if I make the effort. If I have difficulty, I could get help.

Dave's unproductive self-statements can be listed on the right side of Worksheet 1. These can then be contrasted with the unproductive beliefs on the left. Again, note that the productive self-statements are designed to challenge and replace the unproductive thoughts in the left column. The sample work sheet is as follows:

Worksheet 1
Self-Statements/Self-Belief System

Unproductive	**Productive**
1. *Math is impossible.*	1. *It is certainly possible to learn math. Many other people have done it.*
2. *It (math) just can't be done.*	2. *Math is difficult for me and it will require more effort. I can master it if I am willing to try.*
3. *Math shouldn't be so hard.*	3. *The difficulty of a subject has nothing to do with being fair. Some subjects are naturally more difficult than others.*
4. *It's unfair that one subject should be so difficult.*	
5. *Homework is stupid.*	
6. *That (other kids appearing to understand math) just proves how stupid I am.*	4. *Homework is assigned so that you can practice and reinforce what you learn in class.*
7. *That (the A science grade) was just luck.*	5. *Just because other people are listening, it doesn't mean that they aren't having difficulty, nor does it mean that I'm stupid. It just means I'm having trouble understanding math. If I am willing to try, I can understand it.*
8. *Science is easy. If I was smart, math would be easy too.*	
9. *I'll just not do it (homework). It's probably too difficult anyway.*	6. *I received an A in science because I was able to correctly answer the questions. I deserved the A.*
	7. *Science is easier for me than math. Because one subject is more difficult than another doesn't mean I'm not smart.*
	8. *I can probably do the homework if I make the effort. If I have difficulty, I could get help.*

Beside Dave's negative beliefs about himself, he also produced a number of negative thoughts about others, specifically his teacher. These interfered with Dave seeking the help he needed. Again, Dave needs to replace his unproductive beliefs about others with more positive ones. Productive other statements Dave might use are as follows:

1. Teachers want students to learn. That's why they become teachers.
2. Teachers assign homework so students can practice what they learn at home.
3. Teachers realize math is difficult. They are usually willing to give extra help to students who try.
4. Just because people look like they understand, this may not be so. Appearances can be deceiving. Math is difficult for a lot of people, not just me.
5. Inappropriate behavior does not solve my problem. It makes matters worse. It would be better to tell the teacher I am having difficulty. This is more likely to help me solve my problem.

On Worksheet 2, the productive other belief statements would be placed in the right column. These would be used to challenge and replace those in the unproductive column. The completed sample worksheet is as follows:

Worksheet 2
Other-Statement/Other Belief System

Unproductive	**Productive**
1. Teachers are jerks!	1. Teachers want students to learn. That's why they become teachers.
2. They (teachers) just assign homework to ruin your life.	2. Teachers assign homework so students can practice what they learn at home.
3. She (the teacher) probably wouldn't take the time to explain it (homework) to me anyway.	3. Teachers realize math is difficult. They are usually willing to give extra help to students who try.
4. They (other children) probably know what's going on. I'm probably the only one in the whole class who doesn't understand math.	4. Just because people look like they understand, it may not be so. Appearances can be deceiving. Math is difficult for lots of people, not just me.
5. That (Dave's slow moving behavior) will teach her to aggravate me.	5. Inappropriate behavior does not solve my problems. It make matters worse. It would be better to tell the teacher I am having difficulty. That is more likely to help me solve my problem.

If Dave is now able to engage in productive self and other thinking, then his increasing anger, frustration, and depression should become altered as well. Previously on Worksheet 3, Dave's negative emotions were listed in the unproductive column. With Dave's change in thinking, these emotional over-reactions would now be replaced by emotions that could serve as a catalyst for constructive action. The productive emotions are listed on the left hand column of the following sample worksheet. Note how these contrast with those in the right hand column. The productive emotions are less intense and more positive.

Worksheet 3
Affective Self-System

Productive   **Unproductive**

Happy

Cheerful   **Overjoyed**

Focused Energized   _____
Optimism   _____
Hopefulness   _____

Sad

Sorry   **Despair**

_____   *Depression*

_____   _____

Angry

Annoyed   **Furious**

_____   *Increasing anger*

_____   _____

Confused

Undecided   **Overwhelmed**

Uncertain   *Overly frustrated*
Concern   _____

Fear

Nervous   Panic

_____   _____

_____   _____

Dave's unproductive thinking and emotional over-reactions cause him to behave poorly. However, when Dave thinks sensibly and controls his emotions, then appropriate, more focused problem solving behavior is likely to follow. Goal oriented, productive behavior that would facilitate Dave's problem solving capability is as follows:

1. Eye contact with the teacher and the board.

2. Eyes fully open. Face shows an interest in learning.

3. Sitting in the chair properly, facing the teacher and the board.

4. Mouth closed, facial muscles relaxed, normal breathing.

5. Gathering books and materials and moving promptly toward the door.

6. Saying "Yes" when the teacher asks if he was having a problem.

7. Talking in a pleasant, firm tone.

These productive verbal and nonverbal behaviors would be inserted into Worksheet 4 as follows. Note how they contrast with the unproductive behaviors they are designed to replace.

Worksheet 4
Verbal and Nonverbal
Behavior Check List

Nonverbal Coping Behavior

Unproductive

1. A lack of concentration.
2. The narrowing of his eyes and surly look on his face.
3. Sighing.
4. Looking out of the window.
5. Tapping his feet.
6. Putting his head on the desk and pretending to sleep.
7. Moving slowly from his seat to the door.

Productive

1. Eye contact with the teacher and the board.
2. Eyes fully open. Face shows an interest in learning.
3. Sitting in the chair properly facing the teacher and the board.
4. Mouth closed, facial muscles relaxed, normal breathing.
5. Gathering books and materials and moving promptly toward the door.

Verbal Coping Behavior

Unproductive

1. Saying "No" when the teacher asked if he was having a problem.
2. A nasty, defiant tone of voice.

Productive

1. Saying "Yes" when the teacher asks if he is having a problem.
2. Talking in a pleasant, firm tone of voice.

By combining Worksheets 1, 2, 3, and 4, we are able to demonstrate how productive thinking, emotions, and behavior are connected. This enables us to lay the foundation for actually proposing solutions to Dave's problem. Again, for younger elementary school children, the Rob the Robot model might be particularly effective in demonstrating this connection.

Once the connection between Dave's thinking, emotions, and behavior is established, the next step would be to assist Dave in devising a strategy to overcome his difficulty. To do this, we can utilize the material presented in Worksheets 6, 7, and 8.

By using Worksheet 6, we can do a situational analysis in order to identify those factors relevant to solving the problem. These factors, as demonstrated in the following sample of Worksheet 6, are as follows:

Worksheet 6
Situational Formulation and Analysis

1. A description of the problem:

   Dave is frustrated because he does not understand math. He is not concentrating or completing math assignments.

2. The place where it happens:

   The classroom during math class. Dave is not completing assignments at home.

3. Who the participants are:

   Dave and his math teacher.

4. Who says what to whom:

   The teacher asks if Dave is having a problem. Dave says "No."

5. What feeling each person is experiencing:

   Dave is angry, frustrated, and depressed. The teacher is annoyed with Dave's behavior.

6. What each person is thinking:

   Dave blames the teacher and the subject for his problem. Dave believes that he is stupid because he finds math to be difficult. The teacher believes that Dave understands the work and she is confused and irritated by his senseless behavior.

After having analyzed all of these factors, which are impacting on this situation, Dave will then be ready to take constructive action to solve his problem with math. Worksheet 7 can now be used to determine the kind of situation with which Dave must cope. This will be the next step in helping Dave to plan a viable strategy for solving his problem. An examination of Worksheet 7 shows that Dave is confronted with an orienting situation. As the worksheet indicates, orienting situations are those in which you are required to ask for directions, assistance, or information so that you can efficiently and effectively complete a task. In Dave's case, he must obtain assistance in understanding math if he is to successfully complete his assignments. Knowing and understanding that this is an orienting situation will prepare Dave to begin formulating responses, which are most likely to be effective in helping him to acquire the math information he needs.

Dave's next step would be to devise the actual verbal responses that he might use to cope with his particular orienting situation. Specifically, Dave needs math information. An examination of Worksheet 8 shows some sample productive responses to be used and expanded upon. New responses more appropriate for Dave's situation need to be devised.

With regard to the latter, the teacher asked Dave if he was having a problem. Instead of saying "No" and behaving inappropriately, Dave could have made eye contact and said, "Mrs.————, I'm totally confused. Would you please explain the solutions to the math problems again so that I can try to understand them?" Or Dave might state, "I'm sorry Mrs.————, but I don't understand the work. Could we meet after school so you could go over it with me?"

Note Worksheet 8 contains both productive and unproductive sample responses for dealing with an orienting situation. The productive sample responses provide a guide for expressing thoughts in a manner, which is more likely to enable one to effectively solve the problem. The unproductive samples serve as a contrast to emphasize what should not be done. In fact, these are likely to lead to failure. In the following sample, the orienting situation segment from Worksheet 8 has been excerpted and applied to Dave's problem.

Worksheet 8
Productive and Unproductive Verbal Responses for Coping Situations

Orienting Situations

Productive | **Unproductive**

1. Ms. _____, I'm totally confused. Would you please explain the solution to the math problems again so that I can try to understand them?

1. Dave says "No" in a nasty, defiant tone of voice when asked by the teacher if he is having a problem.

2. I'm sorry, Ms. _____, but I don't understand the work. Could we meet after school so that you could go over it with me?

Once the worksheets have been completed, the final portion of the coping skills program can be implemented. Dave could role play the verbal and nonverbal behaviors and obtain appropriate feedback. This will enable him to practice and improve his skill in handling the specific problem confronting him. Once this is refined, he can actually then put it into practice.

Some Suggested Activities

The materials and worksheets in this book can be applied in a number of ways to help children to distinguish between productive and unproductive coping strategies and to learn viable ways to solve life's problems. The following are just a few suggested activities that might be tried to stimulate youngsters in their thinking about productive coping styles and their consequences.

1. Select and analyze newspaper and magazine articles that give quotes or examples of unproductive thinking, emotional over-reactions, or inappropriate behaviors. Productive coping strategies might be selected and analyzed as well. This can also be done with television news clips. In this way, children can visualize some of the productive and unproductive behaviors associated with difficult situations. News clips should be monitored for age appropriateness.

2. Read and discuss biographies and autobiographies in which people have demonstrated effective and ineffective coping styles.

3. Read and discuss children's stories like *The Tortoise and The Hare* or *The Little Engine That Could* and use Rob the Robot in analyzing them.

4. Select movies, cartoons, or television shows in which the main character uses productive thinking and behavior to overcome adversity.

5. Ask members of the community who have coped effectively with a challenge to speak to the class. Police officers, fire fighters, doctors, and business owners would be excellent candidates.

6. Ask classmates to interview each other about a particular situation in which they had to cope. Have children discuss whether the coping behaviors that were chosen were productive or unproductive. The children might then offer other suggestions for turning unproductive responses into productive responses.

7. Write or put on a play/skit in which some person or group of persons face and overcome a problem.

8. Conduct a puppet show using material devised by the children to demonstrate effective and ineffective coping when confronted with a specific problem.

9. Have older students follow stories associated with their current favorite celebrity for a month. Students can report to the class on a challenge that their chosen celebrity has overcome (e.g., rumors, tabloid exploitation) and tell how the celebrity has been working to overcome the problem. Students can then offer suggestions that the celebrity might use to overcome such challenges effectively. This activity should be closely monitored to ensure the appropriateness of the selected events.

10. Identify, read about, and discuss historical figures. Apply their success and failures to the coping strategies model. This can be integrated into the current social studies curriculum.

11. Identify TV commercials and newspaper and magazine articles and advertisements. Focus on how these can influence people's thinking, feeling, and behavior. Discuss the implication of this and how people can prevent themselves form being overly influenced. Apply the coping strategies model when appropriate.

12. Identify a school, community, state, or national problem. Have the children work together in applying the coping strategies model to try and solve the problem.

It should be noted the preceding suggestions are relatively inexpensive to implement. They draw on material and persons who are readily available within the school and community. Most children will find these activities to be stimulating. They can learn much about coping effectively by being keen observers of the media, their school environment, and the people with whom they associate every day. The observations that are gathered will provide a rich source of valuable information.

Bibliography

The following are some sources that might be of assistance in developing a coping strategies program for your school:

Cartledge, G. & Kleefeld, J. (1992). *Taking part: Introducing social skills to children.* Circle Pines, MN: American Guidance Service.

Choen, L. & Frydenberg, E. (1996). *Coping for capable kids: Strategies for parents, teachers, and students.* Waco, TX: Prufrock.

Dacey, J. & Fiore, L. (2000). *Your anxious child: How parents and teachers can relieve anxiety in children.* San Francisco, CA: Jossey-Bass/Pfeiffer.

Dlugokinsk, E.L. & Allen, S.F. (1997). *Empowering children to cope with difficulty and build muscles for mental health.* Washington, DC: Accelerated Development.

Forman, S. (1993). *Coping skills intervention for children and adolescents.* San Francisco, CA: Jossey-Bass/Pfeiffer.

Greenspan, S. (2003). *The secure child: Helping children to feel safe and confident in a changing world.* Cambridge, MA: DeCapo.

Joseph, J. (1994). *The resilient child: Preparing today's youth for tomorrow's world.* New York, NY: Insight Books/Plenum Press.

Lavin, P. (1991). *Teaching kids to think straight.* Columbia, MO: Hawthorne.

Malouff, J. & Schutte, N. (1998). *Games to enhance social and emotional skills.* Sixty-six games that teach children, adolescents, and adults skills crucial to success in life. Springfield, IL: Charles C. Thomas.

Merrell, K. (2001). *Helping students overcome depression and anxiety: A practical guide.* New York, NY: Guilford.

Schiraldi, G. (2001). *The self-esteem workbook.* Oakland, CA: New Harbinger.

Sure, M.B. (1992). *I can problem solve: An interpersonal cognitive problem solving program for children.* Champaign, IL: Research Press.

Zeitlin, S. & Williamson, G.G. (1994). *Coping in young children: Early intervention practices to enhance adaptive behavior and resilience.* Baltimore, MD: Brooks Publishing.

Paul Lavin, Ph.D. and Kathryn Lavin, M.A.